I Belong
Special

**Preparing for
my
First Holy Communion**

In the name
of the
Father

My name is

Florence

Sky Peak

Names

Names are very special.
It is good when we know one another's names.

My friends' names are

If I had a pet spider
I would call it
Legsy

If I had a pet lion
I would call it
Roar

We all get to know Jesus.
We love Jesus more.

My catechist's name is
....

A special person who will pray for me is called

....

The Bible

The Bible tells us about God and people.

Old Testament

Here is a story from the start of the Bible.

God made the world.
He made all the animals.
He asked the man to give each
animal a name.

cat

pig

dog

(Genesis 2:19-20)

Draw your favourite animals or stick fur, leather, wool or smooth scales as different animals.

Penguin

My favourite animal

People wanted to give God a name.

New Testament

The angel said to Mary,
"You will have a baby.
Name him Jesus.
He will be called the Son of God."
(Luke 1:31-32)

The New Testament tells us about Jesus.

John baptised people in the River Jordan.

Those people started a new life.

John felt Jesus was good already.

But Jesus was also baptised to show the way to others.

God said

"This is my Beloved Son."

Colour this picture of Jesus being baptised in the River Jordan by John the Baptist.

Church

I was baptised at

- - - - - - - - - - - - - - - Church.

When I was baptised the priest said to me,

"- - - - - - - - - - -,

I baptise you in the <u>NAME</u> of the Father, and of the Son, and of the Holy Spirit."

When I was baptised God said to me,

"- - - - - - - - - - - -, you are my beloved child. I am delighted with you."

When I go to church I dip my finger in the holy water and say, "In the name of the Father, and of the Son, and of the Holy Spirit."
This is to remind me of my

- -

When I go to the Eucharist I will remember that my baptism links me up with everyone else in church.

We are all baptised.

We are all beloved children of God.
We can all say together:

Our Father, who art in heaven, hallowed be thy name. Thy kingdom come. Thy will be done on earth, as it is in heaven. Give us this day our daily bread, and forgive us our trespasses as we forgive those who trespass against us, and lead us not into temptation, but deliver us from evil.

Everyday Life

The story of Adam tells us that God makes us all, and gives us this beautiful world to care for.
Jesus shows us how to live as children of God.

I can <u>live</u> like a beloved child of God because I <u>am</u> a beloved child of God.
I have the Holy Spirit with me just as Jesus did.

This month I am going to live like a child of God by …

- -

Find all these words about God our Father.

KIND ✓ GENEROUS ✓ PATIENT ✓
LOVING ✓ THOUGHTFUL ✓ FUN ✓
WONDERFUL ✓ CARING ✓

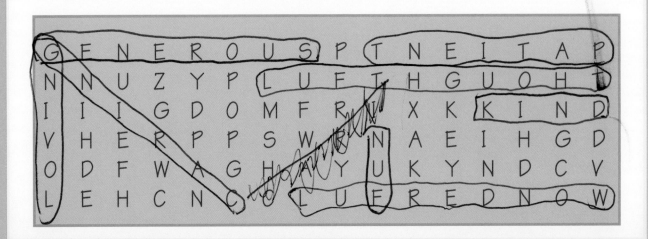

I have called you by your name.

You are mine.

(Isaiah 43:1)

Stick
a
photo
of
yourself
here

This is your page for adding your own ideas. You can use it for drawing pictures, or writing prayers. You might like to stick in a photograph of your baptism.

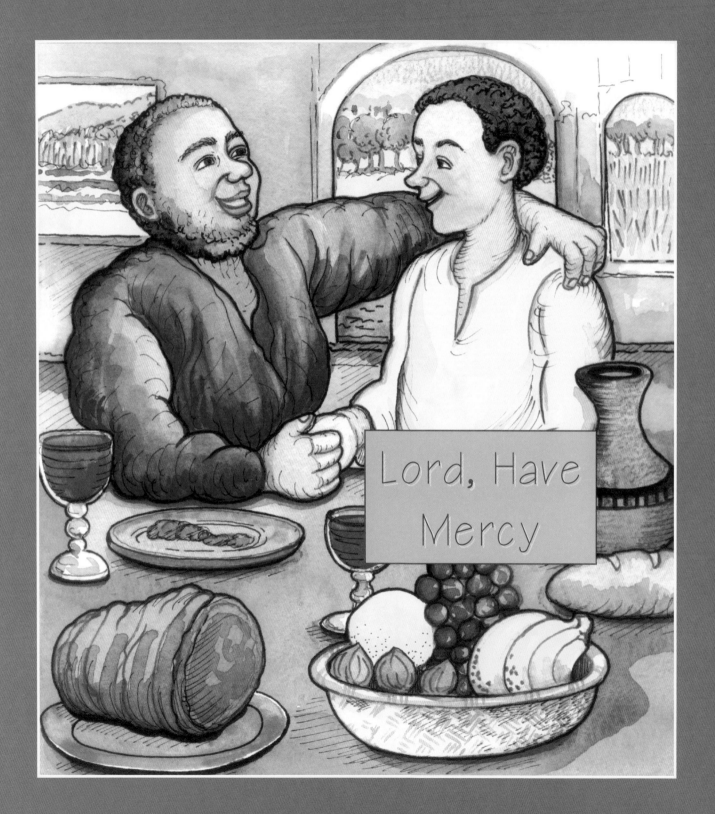

Here is a story about a girl who owned a kitten.

Katie had a for her birthday, but the kitten wouldn't go near her. It hid under the [table].

"Poor thing!" said Katie. "You're cold." And she gave him a [rug]

Still the kitten wouldn't go near her. "Poor thing!" said Katie. "You're thirsty." And she gave him a [bowl] of [milk].

The little kitten still hid. Was Katie angry? Oh no! "Poor thing!" she said. "You're hungry." And she gave him some [food].

And still the little kitten hid. Katie loved her little kitten.

"Poor thing!" she said. "You're very, very frightened."

She gently picked him up and stroked him and stroked him until his little [heart] stopped beating wildly.

"I'm going to call you Holly," she said.

And [kitten] purred and purred.

If you had a kitten that wouldn't go near you what would you do? Would you still love it? Yes

Perhaps you have a pet that was naughty. Tell your friends what the pet did. Do you still love your pet? Yes

Perhaps you are naughty sometimes. Do the grown-ups you belong with still love you? Yes

Draw a picture showing that your family still loves you even after you have been naughty.

God loves us no matter what!

Adam and Eve lived in a lovely garden. God said they could eat anything they liked except the fruit from one tree because it would hurt them.

The crafty snake told Eve she could eat the fruit from this tree.

Eve ate it and shared it with Adam and they were hurt.

God was sad. Adam and Eve were sad. God said, "I will send help for the world."

God kept his promise.

(Adapted from Genesis 3)

Who came to save us?

Jesus!

16

Jesus told stories to teach us about God.

The Forgiving Father

There was once a father who had two sons. The younger son was fed up working for his father.
"Give me my money, Dad," he said.

He left home with the money his father had given him. Soon he had spent it all.

He was sad and hungry. "What shall I do?" he thought. "I know, I'll go back to my father and say sorry."

So he went home.

His father saw him coming
and ran out to hug him.
"I'm sorry," said the
younger son.
"I am just glad to see you
are home," said the
father.

They had a party.
The older son was cross. "I have always stayed with you,"
he said, "but never had a party."

"I love you," said the father. "Everything I
have is yours. Be happy! My son was
lost but now is found!"

(Adapted from
Luke 15:11-32)

We come to God and say,

SORRY.

God is glad to see us.

God is always full of love.

We say,

Lord, have mercy.

Lord   **have**   **mercy**

The father showed mercy to the younger son.
He gave him a party.
God our loving Father shows us mercy.
He gives us Jesus, the Bread of Life.
So we can live as children of God.

Everyday Life

Every time we show mercy, no matter how angry we feel inside, we are learning to be more like God who is always loving and merciful.

How can we show mercy

at home?

Helping Out

at school?

Helping Out

Here is a prayer to say. Choose a word to fill in along the dotted lines. Choose something you would like God to help you with.

Dear Father in heaven,

thank you for your MERCIFUL LOVE.

Help me to be more ......*resilient*...... in future.

I ask this through Jesus Christ

your Son.

Amen.

Don't forget you can add as much as you want to your file.

RECONCILIATION
Celebrating
our Rescue

HIJACKED PLANE LATEST!

EVERYONE RESCUED

"WE ARE DELIGHTED," say families

LOST CHILD RESCUED FROM MOUNTAIN LEDGE

PARENTS OVERJOYED

Have you ever rescued anything that you love very much?
Was it very difficult?

Have you ever seen anyone rescued from a fire or water or from a road accident?
Tell everyone about it.

Perhaps you have been in trouble or danger? Who saved you?
How did you feel afterwards?

Draw a picture of someone being rescued.
It could be a rescue from a fire, or from a storm at sea.

Rescue Story

Once there lived a good man called Daniel. Bad men went to the king and said, "You are the best. No one needs any other god."
The king said, "I am the best, no one needs any other god."

Daniel stayed friends with **the one true God.**
The bad men told the king who was very cross. "I am the best, no one needs any other god!" he shouted and had Daniel given to the lions as lunch.
God rescued Daniel. The lions did not eat him. They went to sleep. Daniel was warm and safe. When the king saw this he believed in **the one true God.**

Daniel's God **saves and rescues.**

Jesus told a story about how God rescues us.

Once a shepherd had one hundred sheep.
He loved them all.
They each had a name.
One day the shepherd saw that one of his

sheep was missing.
"Where is my lost sheep?" he
asked and went to look for it.
He called and searched for the
sheep.
He called it by name.
At last he found the sheep and he brought it safely home.
Then he called all his friends together.
"Let's have a party!" he said. "For I have found my
lost sheep."

If I have nasty feelings I know I need someone to RESCUE me.
God comes to RESCUE me.

Here I am making things right with God's help.

sorry

We say sorry and we are RECONCILED.

RECONCILIATION

We make friends again with people in our lives.

Reconciliation means we forgive.

Reconciliation means God forgives us.

We celebrate God's forgiveness with all God's people.

The priest stands in for the people.

The priest also stands in for God.

When you talk to the priest during Reconciliation it is your SPECIAL TIME.

You can say anything because you are really talking to God your loving RESCUER.

You could say,

I have come to thank God who forgives me

for................... ....

We promise that, with God's help, we will be more loving in future

to ourselves,

to others,

and to God.

How do you feel when God rescues you?

Match the pictures

sorry

love

forgiveness

joy

rescue

help

This is your page for using at home. You might like to draw some pictures of you doing some loving things for God and people. You might like to write a prayer thanking God for rescuing you when you did something unkind.

RECONCILIATION
God Helps Me
Get it Right

Everyday Life

Here I am getting something wrong to start with.

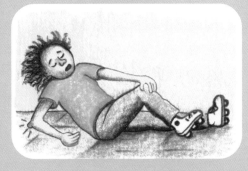

37

**If you are afraid, people who care for you will help you.
They will show they trust you.
You can do it!**

38

Jesus helped people "GET IT RIGHT".
He did this with stories.
Do you remember these stories?

What are they?

Zacchaeus ~ The Man Jesus Believed In

What made Zacchaeus change?

Jesus is with us in a special way in the Sacrament of Reconciliation, just as he and Zacchaeus were together long ago.
We can't see Jesus now, so the priest takes his place.
Zacchaeus loved talking to Jesus. He told him all the things he couldn't tell anyone else, because he knew Jesus would understand.

We can tell the priest anything we are ashamed about, or that we would like to put right. The priest is there to show us Jesus' understanding and love.

HERE IS A RECONCILIATION PRAYER.

We go to Reconciliation for God's help. God can help us put things right.

O my God, thank you for your forgiveness.
I know you love me even when I am unloving.
Please help me to live like Jesus and to forgive others as you forgive me.

Remember that what you say is a secret between you and Jesus. The priest can't tell anyone what you tell him, because he is only standing in for Jesus.

Perhaps you could make up a better prayer. You could say this prayer before you go to sleep at night, and before you go to Reconciliation.

Here is a picture of me, saying that with God's help
I will be more loving in future.
You can draw yourself sitting or kneeling at Reconciliation.

THE SACRAMENT OF RECONCILIATION
Making it right with God.

GETTING READY

Good things and bad things happen.
Remember the things you might have done better.

Say thank you for the times you got things right.

Sometimes we say nasty things or do not do the things we should.
Now we can say sorry to God.

Tell the priest about the times you could have done things better.
He will help you to look at ways to get it right next time.

The priest will then give you a special blessing from God to help you next time.

Penance: Thank God for his love. He forgives you.
Remember to try to listen.
Say the prayer or do the little task the priest asks of you.

44

Look in your Bible.
Jesus helped Peter.

Jesus helped lots of people. Look at these pictures. How did Jesus help these people?

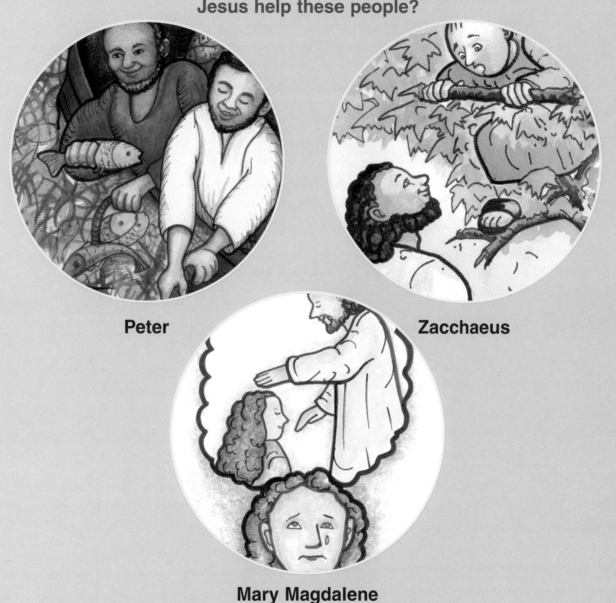

Peter

Zacchaeus

Mary Magdalene

45

Remember: This is YOUR page.

Everyday Life

Here are two special experiences that might happen to you one day.

Which one do you prefer?

The firework display was the best Sarah had ever been to. Rockets zoomed into the sky and showered silver stars above the trees. Catherine Wheels whizzed round and round, and Golden Fountains rained sparkling jewels everywhere.

Andrew felt his heart pounding as he raced for the ball. He reached it just before his opponent, and kicked it with all his might. "Yes!" shouted Andrew. "Goal!" roared the crowd. In the last minute of play Andrew had scored.
His team had won the cup!

Perhaps you have had a much better special experience. Perhaps you dream about something full of glory?

Draw a picture of a *glorious* experience you have had.

All special experiences are gifts from God. Sometimes they are wild and exciting. Sometimes they are peaceful and dreamy. Sometimes the most ordinary things seem somehow different and glorious. All these experiences come from God who makes everything. They all show the GLORY OF GOD.

If you look in your Bible you will find the story of Moses.

He saw the GLORY OF GOD.

Moses looked after the sheep.

Moses took the sheep to Mount Horeb.

Moses saw a bush. It burned but was not hurt.

God spoke to Moses from the bush.

God told Moses who he was and asked Moses to save the people of Israel from slavery.

Moses led the People of Israel to God's Promised Land.

New Testament

For hundreds of years people waited for God to send a Saviour.

In the Temple Simeon waited with Anna.
In her house in Nazareth Mary waited.

Then one day Jesus was born ....

The Shepherds' Story

Colour this picture of the shepherds seeing the glory of God.

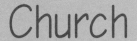

When we go to church for the Eucharist

we are like the shepherds seeing the glory of God.

We sing about God's glory just like the angels.

Glory to God in the highest,
and peace to his people on earth.
Lord God, heavenly King, almighty
God and Father, we worship you, we give
you thanks, we praise you for your glory.

Lord Jesus Christ, only Son of
the Father, Lord God, Lamb of God, you
take away the sin of the world: have
mercy on us; you are seated at the right
hand of the Father: receive our prayer.
For you alone are the Holy One, you
alone are the Lord, you alone
are the Most High,
Jesus Christ, with the
Holy Spirit, in the glory
of God the Father.
Amen.

Everyday Life

Draw three things that make you want to glorify God.

Find the following words in the Word Search:

SUPER ✓ GREAT ✓ LOVE

ADORE ✓ THANK ✓

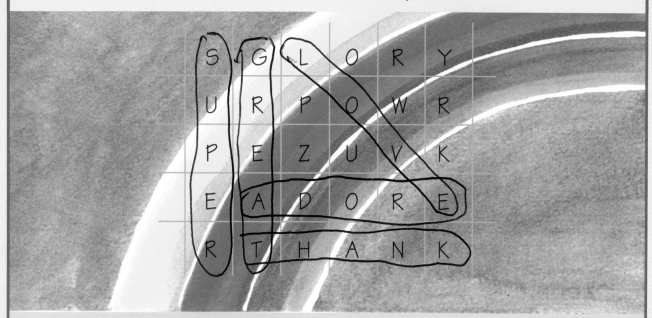

S G L O R Y
U R P O W R
P E Z U V K
E A D O R E
R T H A N K

In church we sing "Hosanna".

We give praise to God.

This space is for your own ideas. You might like to stick in some glorious pictures from a magazine.

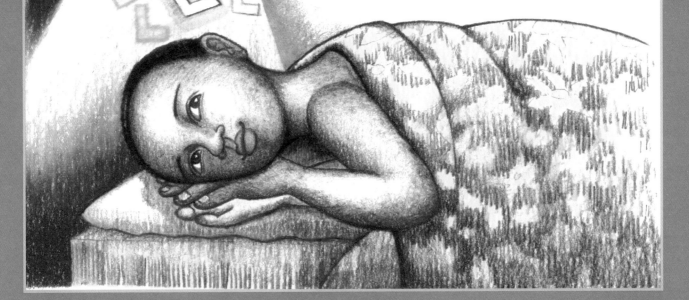

SAMUEL

This is the Word of the Lord

Do you know a good story?

Everyday Life

When we listen we take notice of what we are told.
Who do we listen to?
What do we listen to?

What colour means stop?
What colour means go?

You can colour the pictures.

Listen and feel the sounds.

There are lots of ways to listen.

Some people listen with their ears.

Some people listen with their eyes.

Some people listen with their hands.

We can all listen to God with our hearts.

If we do not listen to people who care about us what happens?
Tell the group about a time you were glad you listened.

Old Testament

Here is the story of Samuel who listened to God. You will find his story in the Old Testament. *(Samuel was a very special child. His mother, Hannah, had prayed to God for a baby for years. She promised God that if she had a baby, she would let him serve God in the Temple when he was old enough. God heard Hannah's prayers, and eventually Samuel was born.)*

When Samuel was still a young boy he went to live and work in the temple. He helped the old priest Eli, who was going blind.

One night when it was very quiet he heard a voice calling him. He thought it was Eli, so he jumped up and ran to him.

"I didn't call you," said Eli. "Go back to bed."

Samuel went back to bed, but he

heard the voice calling him again.
He jumped up and ran to Eli.
"Here I am. I HEARD you call me,"
said Samuel.

"I didn't call you," said Eli. "Go back to bed."

Samuel went back to bed, very puzzled.
He was just falling asleep when he heard the voice
call him for the third time. Up he jumped and ran to Eli.

"You did call me," he said. "I HEARD you."
This time Eli realised that it was God calling Samuel.

"Go back to bed," he said.
"If you hear the voice again, say,
'Speak, Lord, for your servant is listening.'"
Samuel lay down and listened in the silence.
It was a very special time.
Once again God called Samuel.

"SAMUEL! SAMUEL!"

Full of wonder, Samuel said,

"Speak, Lord, for your servant is listening."

God gave Samuel a message for Eli.
It was the first message that Samuel heard from God.
When he grew up he often heard messages from God, and he passed
them on to anyone who would listen.

At last the time came for Jesus to be born.

Was Jesus born rich or poor? Was he born in a stable or a palace?

What do you think?

Jesus is the **WORD OF GOD.**
He told many stories to help us understand.

We can **LISTEN** to the stories in church. The stories are from the Bible. Some stories are from the Old Testament, and the ones about Jesus are from the New Testament.

Have a look in your Bible and see what stories you like best.

Draw you listening to something or someone special. It might be in church, at home, on holiday, or anywhere.

Everyday Life

Here is a game for you to play. When you play it with your catechist you can all move when the catechist throws the dice. When you play it at home everyone can take turns at throwing the dice. I wonder if the best listener will always win!

4 Listen to birds sing. GO FORWARD 4	5	12 Hear good idea. GO FORWARD 6	13	21
	6		14	20
3	7	11	15	16 Hear favourite group. GO FORWARD 2
2	8	10	16	
1 START	9 Listen to good story. GO FORWARD 2		17	18

22

Listen to bad idea.
GO BACK 3

29

30

38

Don't listen to teacher.
GO BACK 4

28

31

37

39

23

27

32

Don't listen
to parent.
GO BACK 5

36

40

24

26

35

41

25

Hear Bible
story.
GO
FORWARD
6

33

34

42

HOME

This page is for your own ideas. You could write a "thank you" prayer for things you like listening to. You could stick in pictures of things that make lovely sounds. How about sausages sizzling in a pan, or your favourite group?

Bread to Offer

Once there was a little . The  shone and made it grow.

It grew into a fine wheat plant with hundreds of .

The  came and cut down the wheat.

She took it to the  to be ground into .

The flour was taken to the to be baked into .

A big  took it to the .

Someone bought the bread and took it home for the .

They made sandwiches and had a great .

Who gets the food in your house?
Who prepares it?
Do you help?

Draw you preparing a meal with people you like. It might be a picnic, or a birthday party, or just a meal you had when everyone was really hungry.

Old Testament

Do you remember the story of Moses?
Do you remember how Moses took the People of God out of Egypt and to the Promised Land?

The people did not know about God. They had to learn how to trust him and how to listen to him.

The people were cross with Moses and God because there was not enough food to eat.

God said, "I will feed them."
He gave them manna like bread from heaven.

"This is the bread which God is giving you to eat," said Moses.

Every day God gave the people food.

Moses saved his people.

But *JESUS IS THE SAVIOUR OF THE WORLD.*

Jesus Feeds 5000 People

Jesus told stories all day.

He healed the sick all day.

Later on people were hungry. The apostles said, "We have no food!"

A boy brought Jesus some bread and fish.

The apostles gave out food when Jesus had blessed it.

Jesus made sure there was enough food for everyone.

There were twelve baskets left over full of food.
Can you count them?

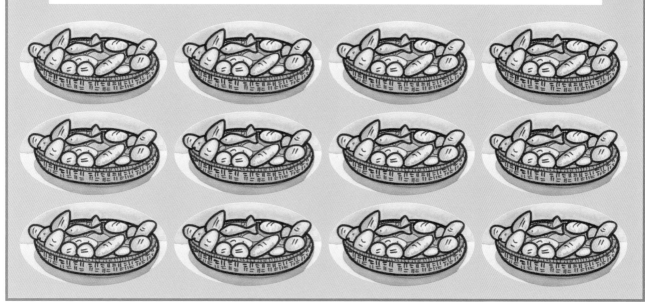

Colour this picture of the boy offering his food to be shared with the crowd.

The prayer of the Mass is called the Eucharist.

The first part is called

THE LITURGY OF THE WORD.

We listen to the stories from the Bible.

The second part of the Eucharist is called

THE LITURGY OF THE EUCHARIST.

The priest says thank you for the gifts of bread and wine.

We thank God for the food we have.

We thank God for all we have.

BLESSED BE GOD FOR EVER

Everyday Life

At Mass remember to say "thank you" for all the good things.

What have you said thank you for?

Remember those who have less than you. Perhaps they have less food or fewer toys, or fewer friends?

What could you do for these people?

Write or draw a picture.

Can you sort out the letters in these words used in church?

ALRAT

CHAEICL

PATNE

BRDAE

WIEN

WARET

Remember to say

thank you   God

Remember: This is YOUR page.

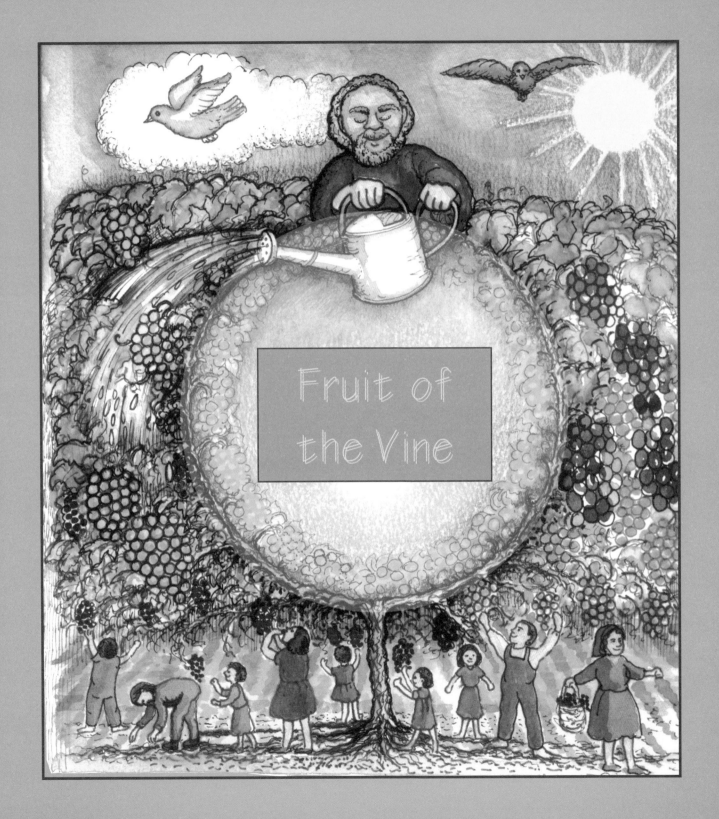

Fruit of
the Vine

Everyday Life

Have you been to a party recently?
What did you have to drink there?

1. Put a tick next to the drinks you had at the party.
2. Colour in all the drinks that grown-ups might have at a party.

85

When we have a party and celebrate, we have a special party drink.

Grown-ups might have a glass of wine.

As we get older we can eat and drink different things or play with different things.

What things do you have at parties?

Draw something you didn't drink when you were a baby, but you do drink now.

Every year the Jewish people celebrate **PASSOVER**.

They remember that God saved them from slavery.

They drink four cups of wine.

The leader of the feast says this prayer as they drink:

"Blessed are you, O Lord our God,
King of the Universe,
Creator of the fruit of the vine."

Where have you heard a prayer like this before?

**Here is a song that Isaiah sang
when the people didn't listen to God**

My friend had a vine-
yard on a very rich hill.
He dug the soil and cleared it of
stones.
He planted the finest vines.
He built a tower to guard them,
dug a pit for treading the grapes.
He waited for the grapes
to ripen, but every grape
was sour.

(Isaiah 5:1-2)

87

Later on, Isaiah wrote this:

The Lord will say this of
his pleasant
vineyard.
"I watch over it and water it all the
time. I guard it night and day so
that no one will harm it...
In days to come the people of
Israel will take root like a tree,
and they will bud. The earth will
be covered with the fruit
they produce."

(Isaiah 27:2-6)

**Jesus loved to celebrate. He loved to go to parties.
One day Jesus and his mother were invited to a wedding in a town called Cana.**

Mary and Jesus are invited to a wedding. They go to a wedding in a town called Cana...

The wine starts to run out.

She tells the servants, "Do whatever he asks you to."
Jesus asks the servants to fill the jars with water from the well...

Jesus turns the water into wine...

Everyone was happy.

Colour this picture of the wedding feast of Cana.

Church

When we go to the Eucharist there is so much to think about:

The past…
Moses.

**Now…
Jesus
saves the
world.**

The
present…
**Jesus with
me.**

**For ever…
Peace in
the future.**

**God has always loved his people.
In heaven there is no sin or sadness.
When we receive Holy Communion we can think about heaven.
Jesus spoke about it as an everlasting party.**

*I am the vine, you are the branches.
We are God's vineyard.*

Now God's home is with his people.
He will wipe all tears from their eyes.

(Revelation 21)

Everyday Life

Say "thank you" to God for being with you.

At **THE LAST SUPPER** Jesus said the bread and wine was himself.

Jesus called the hard times of his life a **CUP OF SORROW.**

Doing what is right can be hard sometimes but Jesus asks us to try to
stand up for what is right.
We might find this hard at first but we will be bringing
God's everlasting party.

THE ETERNAL BANQUET

In the Eucharist we join our love with Jesus' unselfish love,

"No one has greater love than to give up his life for his friends."

Here is a Word Search. Find all these words:

FEAST   PARTY   KINGDOM
LOVE   HAPPINESS
WINE   VINE   BRANCHES
DRINK   CUP

L	O	V	E	Z	M	H	A	P	P	I	N	E	S	S	J
V	C	I	Z	Y	P	L	K	A	Y	T	R	Q	W	X	J
K	I	N	G	D	O	M	F	R	F	X	K	N	I	R	D
G	H	N	M	P	P	S	W	T	S	A	E	F	H	G	D
B	D	F	E	U	G	H	K	Y	L	K	Y	T	D	C	V
S	E	H	C	N	A	R	B	Y	H	J	K	E	N	I	W

Remember: This is YOUR page. You could stick in some happy pictures of our beautiful world. You could stick in some sad pictures showing what still needs to be done to bring about the Kingdom of God.

Do this in Memory of Me

Everyday Life

We have lots of different kinds of meals.

We have [ ]
RATPIES

We have [ ]
KATE WAYAS

We have [ ]
CIPNICS

We have [ ]
MAIFLY MELAS

We have [ ]
CUBEBEARS

A really good meal is one where we enjoy the food and enjoy the company.
We are changed for the better after a really good meal.

Draw a picture of a really good meal you had. Can you remember what you ate and drank? Can you remember what you talked about?

Moses led the People of God out of slavery.

The people ate a very quick meal, but it was very special. It was for the journey to freedom.
They made bread quickly, and without yeast.

They ate lamb with herbs.

That night the angel passed over the cities of Egypt.

Every year the People of Israel remember this PASSOVER meal to remind them that God was their SAVIOUR.

New Testament

Jesus celebrated the **Passover** every year. When he was a boy he asked questions about it, and learnt what it all meant.

He realised how important it was. It celebrated how the People of God were saved from sin and death. Their lives were changed from lives of slavery to lives of freedom.

Jesus spent his whole life telling people how much God loved them. It is difficult to understand that some people hated him. These people decided to kill him. Jesus knew he was going to die. The reason he had come from heaven was to give his life for us. This was how he was going to save us. By dying and rising from the dead he showed us that death and evil had no power over him, and need have no power over us. Jesus is the new

LAMB OF GOD.

Jesus didn't just give his life for us years ago when he died on Calvary. He gives us his new risen life now. He did this by changing the **Passover** feast into the **Eucharist.**

The **Eucharist** is the new **Passover** of the new People of God.

Jesus is the new Lamb of God who saves us and brings us life.

THE LAST SUPPER

The night before he died, Jesus met with his friends to celebrate the Passover feast.
Judas, who was going to betray Jesus, was there.
Jesus loved all his friends, even Judas.

While they were at the table, Jesus took bread, blessed it, broke it, and gave it to his friends. He said,

TAKE – EAT. THIS IS ME.

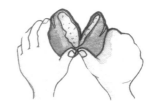

Then he took the wine. He gave thanks, and told them to share the cup. He said,

TAKE – DRINK. THIS IS ME.

He told them to do what he had done. Whenever they did this, Jesus would be really there, as food and drink from heaven.

Colour this picture of the Last Supper.

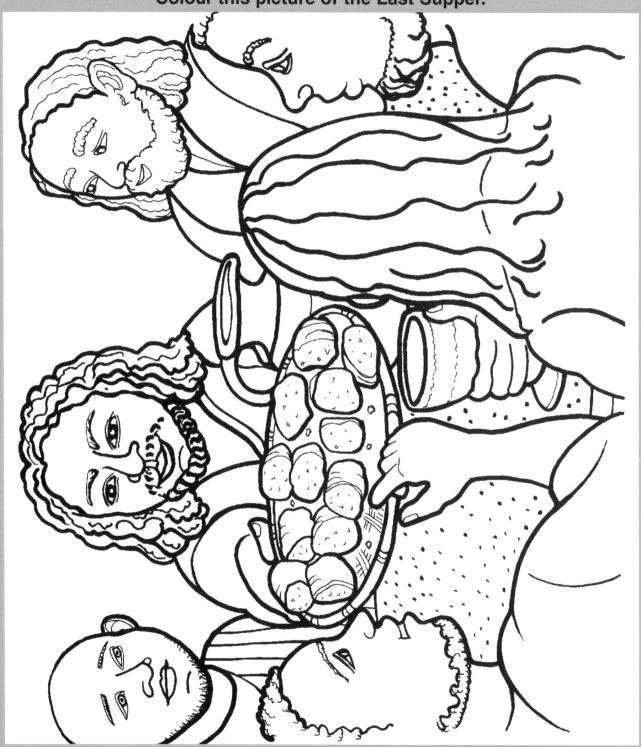

At the Eucharist the Last Supper of Jesus is taking place all over again. The priest says the words of Jesus,

TAKE AND EAT – TAKE AND DRINK.
THIS IS ME.

The bread isn't ordinary bread any more. It is Jesus – the Bread of Life.

The wine isn't ordinary wine any more. It is the life of Christ.

This is Jesus who gave his life for us.

Jesus makes us strong to LOVE.

LOVE is the most important reason why Jesus gives us himself in the **Eucharist**.

- ## JESUS LOVES US
- ## HE WANTS US TO LOVE HIM AND EVERYONE

Everyday Life

Jesus shares his life with us.
You will have more strength to love as Jesus does.

Jesus is with you no matter what problems you face.
You have the life and love of Christ in you.

Quiz

What did Jesus give his
friends at the Last Supper?
a) steak and chips
b) bread and wine
c) coke and crisps

What was the festival Jesus
and his friends were taking
part in?
a) Passover
b) Christmas
c) Yom Kippur

What did Jesus say at the
Last Supper?
a) Take this and eat it – I will
never cook for you again.
b) Take this and eat it – this is
me.
c) Eat this food and then I'm
leaving you on your own.

Who gave his life for you
because he loves you so much?
a) A famous actor
b) Your teacher
c) Jesus

Where was Jesus sent to die?
a) Herod's dungeon
b) Calvary
c) Bethlehem

REMEMBER to make this page special by adding bits of your own.

Body of Christ

Everyday Life

Have you ever seen a tadpole turning into a frog?
First the back legs grow. Then the front legs grow.

Its long tadpole tail disappears.
Soon it can hop and live on land.

The same life is inside the little creature, but it looks completely different on the outside.

Caterpillars change as well.
At first the caterpillar is fat and crawly.
It creeps along branches and twigs.
Sometimes it falls to the ground.

After sleeping in a cocoon it rises to a new life as a butterfly.

Colour in this butterfly with its beautiful new wings.

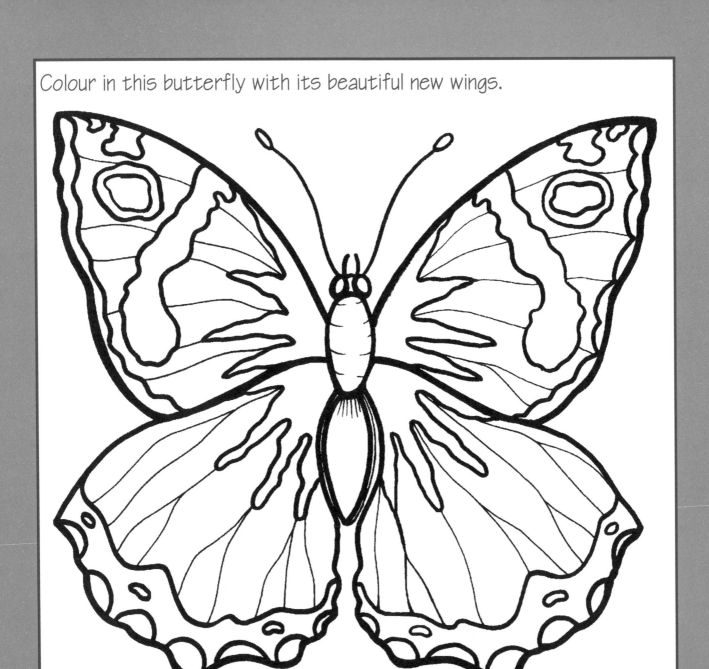

You have also changed on the outside since you were born. The change in you is a gradual change. Now you are bigger and stronger than when you were a baby. But you probably feel the same inside as you did a few years ago. You are the same person.

Old Testament

There are no Old Testament stories this time. Jesus came to bring about the New Testament.

This time we have two true stories about after Jesus had died and been buried. They are about Jesus risen from the dead.

New Testament

Last time we talked about the day before Jesus died. He gave himself to his friends as food and drink at his Last Supper. The next day he was put to death on the cross.

He was laid in the tomb.

His friends thought it was all over and they were sad.

On Saturday he was still dead. A guard was at the tomb.

But on Sunday he was alive again!

Lots of people saw him but he looked so different that they did not recognise him.

Mary and the Gardener

Mary was a friend of Jesus. She remembered how he had helped her.

On the Sunday morning Mary took special spices to put on Jesus' body. But the stone had been moved and the tomb was empty.

Seeing a man she thought was a gardener Mary asked, "Have you taken Jesus away?"

The gardener said, "Mary". He smiled. It was Jesus. He was alive with a new risen life!

Colour this picture of Jesus and Mary Magdalene.

Two Friends and a Stranger

Two friends of Jesus were very sad because Jesus had died. They left Jerusalem to go to Emmaus, a town near by.

On their way they were joined by another man. "Why are you sad?" he asked them.

They told him about how Jesus had been killed. It meant that all they had hoped for was finished.

"Don't be silly," said the man, "I will explain." And he told them all about the things the prophets had said.

When they reached the village the friends asked the stranger to join them for something to eat.

At the table the stranger took some of the bread and broke it. "It is true!" cried the two friends. "This is Jesus. He is alive!"

Jesus is alive

Church

When we go to the Eucharist we really meet Jesus just as Mary Magdalene and the two friends did.

Jesus isn't there with a physical body, like the one he had before he died, but we really do meet him in a special way when we go to Communion.

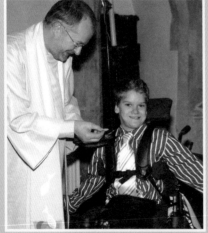

When the priest says the words of consecration,

"THIS IS MY BODY"
"THIS IS THE CUP OF MY BLOOD"

the Holy Spirit enters the bread and wine with the risen life of Christ.

When we receive the bread the priest says,

"THE BODY OF CHRIST."

We say,

"AMEN." (Yes, we believe.)

When we receive the cup the priest says,

"THE BLOOD OF CHRIST."

We say,

"AMEN." (Yes, we believe.)

Everyday Life

When we receive Jesus in Holy Communion we are united with him in a special way. We are changed. The risen life of Christ is in us.

WE ARE THE BODY OF CHRIST.

Finish this prayer:

Dear Jesus,

thank you for coming to me in the Eucharist...

Next time we meet, we will be thinking about all we can do to carry on the Good News that Jesus gives us.

Make this page special by adding bits of your own.

To Love and
to Serve

Everyday Life

Every day you are lucky enough to have something to eat.

Draw your favourite food and drink.

If you don't eat you feel - - - - (weka)

You might even - - - - - (fanit)

Draw you feeling weak before a meal and full of energy after a meal.

Me feeling weak before a meal.   Me full of energy after a meal.

Old Testament

In the desert God fed them.

Moses led the People of Israel out of slavery.

Joshua took the people into the Promised Land.

Then, when Moses was going to die, he asked Joshua to lead the people.

Joshua means SAVIOUR.
Jesus means SAVIOUR too.
In their new home the people remembered to share what they had, and if they ever forgot about God there were the prophets to remind them.

Then came JESUS
THE SON OF GOD.

Jesus is a prophet, but he is much more than a prophet. Jesus is the

SON OF GOD.

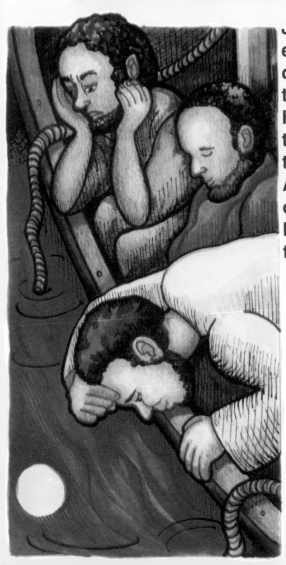

Jesus, the Son of God, spent his life on earth showing us how to live as children of God. Jesus was always kind to the poor people.

He healed the sick, fed the hungry, he told everyone how much God loved them.

After he rose from the dead he carried on loving everyone. Here is a story of how he fed his friends when they were tired and hungry.

One evening Peter was bored. He said to his friends, "I'm going fishing." His friends said, "We'll come with you." They got their old boat out, and dragged it into the lake. They fished all night, but they couldn't catch anything. Not even an old sandal!

When the sunrise came they were cold and hungry. They decided to go

home. They were very disappointed. Now they would have to buy some food for their breakfast. They could see a stranger on the shore. The stranger called out to them, "Have you caught anything?"

"No," they called back to the stranger.

"Cast your net on the other side of the boat," shouted the stranger.

"Then you will find some fish." They cast their net, and, to their surprise, they caught so many fish that they could not pull the net on board.

"It's the Lord!" shouted John. When Peter heard this, he jumped overboard to get to Jesus.

When everyone else had landed, they noticed that Jesus had a fire already lit, and he was cooking a lovely breakfast for them on the beach.

Colour this picture of Jesus with food for his friends at the seaside.

Church

At the end of the Eucharist, the priest or deacon says,

"The Mass has finished.
Go out, to love and serve the Lord. We have been fed by our
Good Shepherd. Now we have a chance to show how much
we love him. We have a chance to copy him, by loving
and serving everyone we meet."

Here are some ways you can love and serve
the Lord during the week:

help someone older than you

do the gardening

look after baby

visit someone sick

Write a letter to your Prayer Sponsor saying thank you for praying for you.
Here is some help with ideas and spelling:

Dear ....

Thank you very much for praying for me.

enjoyed   First Holy Communion   lovely weather   excited
nervous   very happy   family   relations   presents   tired

I hope you are keeping well.

Love

Here is your last Word Search. Have fun doing it, and enjoy belonging to the new People of God for the rest of your life.
The words you are looking for are:

HAPPINESS CHRIST CONTENTMENT STRENGTH

MASS LORD LIFE

```
H  A  P  P  I  N  E  S  S  G  H  J  K  A  T  L
H  Y  G  T  L  R  I  P  E  T  S  I  R  H  C  O
S  W  N  H  T  G  N  E  R  T  S  S  E  V  H  R
S  K  R  B  V  S  Z  M  V  H  T  I  E  F  T  D
A  D  H  M  N  E  X  L  E  X  C  Z  W  Q  I  W
M  E  T  N  E  M  T  N  E  T  N  O  C  M  A  L
```

**THANKS
BE
TO
GOD**

131

Make this page special by adding bits of your own. You could add pages and pages of things if you wanted to. It could be a place where you collect prayers and ideas about God and people and everything God has made.

My Prayers

Sign of the Cross
In the name of the Father,
and of the Son,
and of the Holy Spirit.
Amen.

The Lord's Prayer
Our Father, who art in heaven,
hallowed be thy name;
thy kingdom come;
thy will be done on earth as it is in
heaven.
Give us this day our daily bread;
and forgive us our trespasses
as we forgive those
who trespass against us;
and lead us not into temptation,
but deliver us from evil.
Amen.

Hail Mary

Hail, Mary, full of grace,
the Lord is with you.
Blessed are you among women,
and blessed is the fruit
of your womb, Jesus.
Holy Mary, Mother of God,
pray for us sinners,
now and at the hour of our death.
Amen.

Glory be to the Father

Glory be to the Father and to the Son and to the Holy Spirit,
as it was in the beginning, is now, and ever shall be,
world without end.
Amen.

Grace before Meals

Thank you, Lord, for this food
and for the work of those who prepared it.
Bless us as we share your gifts.
Amen.

Prayer of Thanksgiving

Thank you, Lord, for all your gifts to me.
Help me to use them in your service.
Amen.

Trinity Prayer
Glory to the Father, and to the Son,
and to the Holy Spirit.
As it was in the beginning, is now,
and will be for ever.
Amen.

The Apostles' Creed
I believe in God, the Father almighty,
creator of heaven and earth.
I believe in Jesus Christ, his only Son, our Lord.
He was conceived by the power of the Holy Spirit
and born of the Virgin Mary.
He suffered under Pontius Pilate,
was crucified, died and was buried.
He descended to the dead.
On the third day he rose again.
He ascended into heaven,
and is seated at the right hand of the Father.
He will come again to judge the living and the dead.
I believe in the Holy Spirit,
the holy catholic Church,
the communion of saints,
the forgiveness of sins,
the resurrection of the body,
and the life everlasting.
Amen.

Eucharistic Responses

Penitential Rite

Priest:	…Lord, have mercy.
People:	Lord, have mercy.
Priest:	…Christ, have mercy.
People:	Christ, have mercy
Priest:	…Lord, have mercy.
People:	Lord, have mercy.

Liturgy of the Word

After the first reading:

Priest:	This is the Word of the Lord.
People:	Thanks be to God.

Before the gospel:

Priest:	The Lord be with you.
People:	And also with you.
Priest:	A reading from the holy gospel according to…
People:	Glory to you, Lord.

After the reading of the gospel:

Priest:	This is the gospel of the Lord.
People:	Praise to you, Lord Jesus Christ.

Sign of Peace

Priest:	The peace of the Lord be with you always.
People:	And also with you.

The priest invites the people to give the sign of peace.

Priest:	Let us offer each other the sign of peace.

At Mass we exchange a sign of peace by shaking hands with those around us and by saying: Peace be with you.

Eucharistic Acclamation

Priest: ...Let us proclaim the mystery of faith:

People: Christ has died,
Christ is risen,
Christ will come again.

or

People: Dying you destroyed our death,
rising you restored our life.
Lord Jesus, come in glory.

or

People: When we eat this bread
and drink this cup,
we proclaim your death, Lord Jesus,
until you come in glory.

or

People: Lord, by your cross and resurrection
you have set us free.
You are the Saviour of the world.

Rite of Communion

People: Lord, I am not worthy to receive
you, but only say the word and I
shall be healed.

Dismissal

Priest: Go in peace to love and serve the Lord.
People: Thanks be to God.

Special Words

Baptism ~ At my baptism I became a member of God's Christian family, the Church.

Body of Christ ~ A name for Holy Communion and also a name for the family of the Church.

Bread of Life ~ A name for the sacrament of Jesus in Holy Communion.

Eucharist ~ Means thanksgiving.

*At the Last Supper Jesus asked us to **"Do this in memory of me."***
Jesus took bread and wine, he blessed it, he broke the bread and gave the bread and wine to his disciples to eat and drink.
When we gather together to celebrate the Eucharist we do what Jesus asked us to do: we take the gifts of bread and wine, we bless them, the priest breaks the bread, and at Communion he gives us Jesus under the appearance of bread and wine.

Eucharistic Prayer ~ The prayer which is at the heart of the Mass when our gifts of bread and wine are blessed and we are reminded that Jesus lived, died, and rose from the dead so that we can share life for ever.

Gospel ~ The Good News of Jesus Christ.

Holy Communion ~ This is the moment when we receive Jesus under the appearance of bread and wine.

Host ~ The wafer of bread which is consecrated by the priest in the Eucharistic Prayer.

Lamb of God ~ A name Christians give to Jesus.

Last Supper ~ The special meal which Jesus shared with his friends the night before he died.

Liturgy of the Word ~ The part of the Mass when we listen to readings from the Bible.

Preparation of Gifts ~The time during the Eucharist when we prepare and bring gifts of bread and wine forward in procession to offer as signs of our world which are to be changed into the sacrament of Jesus present in a special way amongst us.

Sign of Peace ~ A sign of love and friendship, usually a handshake, by which we wish one another the peace of Christ.

MEMO

These people were present to celebrate my
First Communion Day with me

I received Holy Communion for the first time on

_____

at

_____

Celebrant

_____

My catechist

_____

My parent/s

_____